AF479844

Love Notes

Affirmations, Essays,
Inspirational Notes, Poems, and
Quotes Inspired for Healing

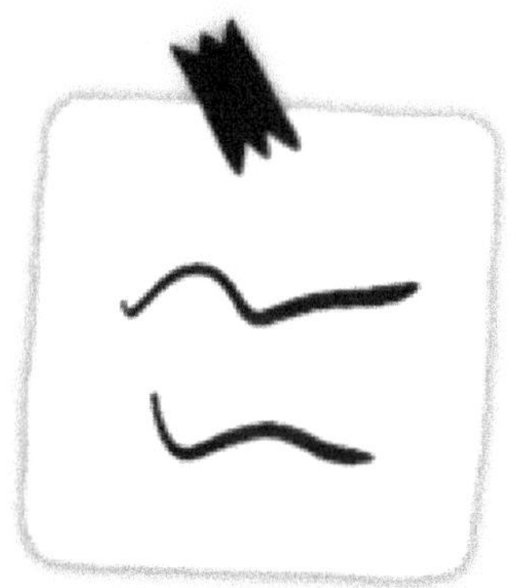

By

Cherice N. Carter

Cherice N. Carter

Love Notes: Affirmations, Essays, Inspirational Notes,

Poems, and Quotes Inspired for Healing

Copyright © 2024 by Cherice N. Carter

Cover Design by Daine DuPree

Print ISBN#979-8-218-34975-2

Printed in United States of America

First Edition: March, 2024

Bibliography

Merriam-Webster. "Merriam-Webster.com Dictionary."
Merriam-Webster. https://www.merriam-
webster.com/dictionary.

Bible Gateway. "Holy Bible: New International Version." Bible
Gateway. https://www.biblegateway.com.

Acknowledgments

I dedicate this book to my God, who created me to become His Source to pour life into those who need encouragement. I thank God for my purpose. He gently guided me on this path to share His never-ending love. From whom every breath emerges and to whom every whisper returns, You, who crafted galaxies with mere thoughts and birthed stars with gentle words, entrusted me with the sacred quill of healing, a gift undeterred.

In Your infinite wisdom, You carved me as a vessel to channel Your grace, speak life into lonely places, wrestle with wounds unseen, bind broken spirits with words woven tight, and be a beacon, a reflection of Your eternal light. For the gift of writing that mends, uplifts, and renews, for the words that flow, inspired by divine cues, I am humbly indebted. My gratitude knows no bounds, for in Your purpose, my true calling resounds. May this book testify to Your boundless grace, a symphony of hope, love, and solace.

For the souls seeking refuge, a sanctuary in written form, crafted not by my hand, but by Yours, ever warm. With reverence and love, I offer this dedication to You, the Source of all creation and inspiration. May every word heal as You intended it to be, a testament to Your love and a reflection of Your decree.

Your child,

Cherice

To Ryan and RJ,

My children are the shining stars in my universe, whose laughter echoes as the most harmonious melodies and whose dreams pave the path to a brighter tomorrow. You are the inspiration behind every word and the heartbeat that gives life to every page. May this book serve as a testament to my unwavering love for you and as a reminder that every challenge faced and every story penned is to build a legacy you'll be proud to inherit.

You will always be the light in my life that will shine forever.

With all my love,

Mommy

To Mommy and Daddy,

You sacrificed your wants and needs for me to live without being deprived of anything life could offer me to succeed. Your roots have anchored me through life's storms. Your teaching is evident today. I could not see the forest for the trees when I was a young girl, but I can see the forest clearly as an adult. I understand why you were pushing me to see the best in myself. Thank you for everything.

Your loving daughter,

Cherice

To my siblings,

You have grown alongside me, shading, supporting, and shaping our collective journey. Each of you have counseled me. In the story of my life, you are the characters who have added depth, emotion, and lessons. This book is a whisper of my gratitude, a testament to the enduring love and strength you've gifted me. For every word written and every dream chased, I owe a piece to each of you.

With deepest gratitude and love,

Cherice

To my nieces and nephews,

I cherish our precious memories and look forward to creating more of them with you. You were my first babies that helped shape the mother I am today. Each of you has marked your spot in this world. Every mark you left has shown your persistence to succeed. I am honored to be your auntie.

Love,

Auntie Cherice

To my aunts and uncles,

You have shared countless family stories that are in our family's DNA. Thank you for loving me!

Love,

Cherice

To my cousins,

My first friends and partners in mischief, you have been there for me. Your doors are always open for me to walk through without judgment. We have fought, cried, and laughed so many times together. Our bond will never break the roots that our ancestors planted.

Love for always and forever,

Cherice

To my dear Aunt Penny,

A guiding star whose wisdom has highlighted paths unknown. Your counsel has shaped my soul's voyage. You've been the compass when I felt lost, the solace in times of doubt, and the beacon that led me to deeper understandings. You have always been there for advice. I am thankful for your truthfulness during my spiritual journey.

With profound love and respect,

Cherice

To my godmothers,

Jo Ellyn Johnson, Patricia Johnson, and Linda Simms, I appreciate your wisdom and guidance. You are dynamic in your unique way. Each of you has a radiant beauty that shines inward and outward. I love you.

Your goddaughter,

Cherice

To my cherished friends,

Who saw the light in me when darkness closed my vision,

Who whispered words of encouragement when doubt echoed loudly,

Who held me up when I felt like falling.

You are the force that propels me forward,

The gentle nudge when I stand at a crossroads, hesitant,

The laughter that breaks the monotony of hard days,

And the belief that reinforces my every step.

This book is a testament to persistence and dreams,

That are intertwined with your unwavering faith.

For every page written, there's a memory of our journey,

For every story told, there's a piece of your heart.

May this dedication stand as a humble token

Of my profound gratitude and eternal love.

Your sister forever,

Cherice

To the spiritual souls who have guided, nurtured, and inspired,

The late Reverend Cornelius Parker, whose wisdom was like an ever-burning torch, lighting the darkest corners of doubt with unwavering faith. You were the first spiritual leader that showed me how to love and know God. I first felt God's presence in your church at age four.

Pastor William Griffin, whose compassion was a boundless sea, touching every shore with kindness, grace, and humility. You provided the necessary tools to continue my faith journey. Thank you for everything.

The late Bishop Arthur M. Brazier, a pillar of strength whose legacy of leadership and vision resounds in every echoing sermon. You were there for me during my time of need. I am forever grateful for your kindness and delicate care during my storm.

Evangelist Ivory Nuckolls is a dedicated servant to God. Your counsel taught me not to lean to my understanding. You listened with an empathic ear while I peeled off layers of myself. I am eternally grateful to you.

Dr. Horace E. Smith, MD, a beacon of both science and spirit, who taught us that healing is both an art and a commitment. You have dedicated your life to teaching the word of God. Your fiery passion for teaching God's word always comes through during your sermons. Thank you for sharing your passion for God.

Pastor John F. Hannah, whose passion for service ignites souls, reminding us of the transformative power of love and purpose. You are funny, charismatic, intelligent, and a profound leader. I am thankful God led me to your teachings.

And Pastor Jermone Glenn, a visionary of contemporary times, who seamlessly bridges tradition with the urgencies of today. You and Pastor Hannah can bring the church to its knees with your impeccable teachings.

Each one has been "the" spiritual constellation of my life, bestowing wisdom, love, and guidance in times of strife.

This book stands as a humble tribute to the divine path they've created, the souls they've touched, and the spirits they've saved.

It has been an honor to be their student. Their teachings have each word spoken etched in my heart. I dedicate these pages to this woman and men of God. I am blessed to experience each of these spiritual giants.

Your loving student,

Cherice

To my ancestors,

Stolen from their land, gathered and shackled like cattle, and placed on a boat to sail at sea to reach shores your eyes never seen. Your journey to America was not your vision. Living in captivity did not stop your path. The strength you showed during that time was passed down to your future. Love lived inside you throughout your trials and tribulations despite the brutality meant to break your spirit.

You saw hope when there was despair, joy when there was misery, calmness when there was fear. Your courage soared during unbearable tests of inequities, injustice, and denial of your heritage and culture. The intolerable suffering you endured has not been in vain. Your legacy is a testament to God's promise.

I thank God for your perseverance. You passed down lessons my late grandparents, uncles, and aunts shared with me. I am grateful for every conversation eloquently drafted by you. From your mouth to your children's ears, these conversations will undoubtedly continue for years.

You visualized freedom for future generations. Your dedication and drive taught your lineage dreams can become a reality. I can attest your vision has come true. Your lineage is filled with doctors, lawyers, politicians, business owners, religious clergy, presidents and vice presidents of companies, and authors who are game changers.

We owe you for the paths you walked and illuminated to give us a place in this world that was not kind to you. Your tenacity shaped each of our desires to walk in our purpose. Therefore, every word I write, every idea I have, and every business venture I enter directly results from your resilience and grace. I am indebted to you forever. Thank you for my life!

Sincerely, your dream carrier and curse breaker,

Cherice

Contents

INTRODUCTION   19

CHAPTER 1: SELF-AFFIRMATION   21

CHAPTER 2: SPIRITUALITY   53

CHAPTER 3: RELATIONSHIPS 75

CHAPTER 4: GRIEF   97

CHAPTER 5: MOTIVATON   112

Introduction

A story is waiting to be told in every whisper of the wind and each leaf rustle. Words have the inexplicable ability to touch souls, mend broken hearts, and reignite the dimming embers of hope.

"Love Notes" is a culmination of that very essence, where words become more than just letters on a page; they become pathways to healing. Nothing is more meaningful than gathering your thoughts with inspirational words to help others. Words are compelling and can transcend the feelings of people.

This collection isn't merely a compilation of thoughts but a journey through the varied landscapes of the human heart: from the affirmations we tell ourselves in the mirror to the spiritual bonds that tether us, from the intricacies of relationships to the silent echoes of grief, from the fires of motivation to the shadows of illness. To the all-encompassing embrace of love— every chapter in this book seeks to address the facets of life that make us, break us, and remake us.

There's a profound beauty in seeking solace through words. They offer companionship in loneliness, strength in vulnerability, and understanding in confusion. I have used words to comfort family and friends when they need inspiration. My vision is that "Love Notes" serves as that quiet friend who understands without judgment, guiding you back to a place of love and self-acceptance.

To love another, we must first embark on the journey of self-love. As you flip through these pages, may you find the inspiration to love yourself more than yesterday, recognizing that the most valid form of love springs from within.

I want to be the light for those who only see darkness. Always be the light in the room. Your light can make a difference in someone's life. ♥

May "Love Notes" be your beacon on this journey of self-discovery and healing.

CHAPTER 1

Self-Affirmation

self-affirmation
noun

self-af·fir·ma·tion   self-ˌa-fər-ˈmā-shən

plural: self-affirmations

a: the act of affirming one's own worthiness and value as an individual for beneficial effect (such as increasing one's confidence or raising self-esteem)

Do you ever ask yourself, "Who am I?" I do. The only way that I stay grounded is through my faith, prayers, and daily affirmations. We must affirm who we are every day. No one can evaluate or value us, as it is our divine order to assess who we are. There is only one being that has authority over us. That's God. He created us for His purpose and in His image. We gripe about not being in a place where we feel solidified. Well, speak life over yourself. Self- affirmations are key to defining your path.

Self-affirmations are required to arrive at your destiny. If we do not affirm ourselves, who will? The first sentence after prayer in the morning should be a self-affirmation. Trust me, this will order your steps for the day. If you do not have any self-affirmations written down, take time to create at least five for your life. We must speak life into our aspirations.

When you are questioning your worth, recite Jeremiah 29:11: "For I know the plans I have for you," declares the LORD, "plans to prosper you and not to harm you, plans to give you hope and a future." Keep winning love from yourself. Pour into your cup to create a future directed just for you.

Prayer for Self-Affirmations

- 23 -

Dear Heavenly Father, we lift your name in the midst of our storm. You are the Alpha and Omega. You are the author of our life. You have given me favor over those who wanted to defeat me. You hold the keys to all the doors that were commanded to open for me. You have given me peace when in doubt. Today, I shall affirm my life will be for my purpose. God continues to order my steps. I no longer will second-guess my journey. You have guided me to righteousness.

In Jesus' name. Amen

My destiny is only tied to God!

I will examine my financial choices to secure a debt-free future.

I will never be bound by anyone again.

I am beautiful, intelligent, creative, and sassy!

I was created to pour life into others. Therefore, I must pour life into myself. I can't pour from a half-empty cup.

I will evaluate every relationship to ensure there is value.

I will open my heart to love, cherish, and adore my future love.

I will look for opportunities that will be a long-term investment in my life.

I will take ownership of my happiness every day. My happiness is my responsibility.

I am the force created to impact lives. My gift shall reign over all those who speak against me. I am a survivor that will beat all odds. I shall not be afraid of the wars raging against me. I have decided to take back my life. Nothing can stop me. I am unstoppable!

I will only speak life over me. There is power in using my tongue. Nothing shall cross my threshold that will negatively impact me.

I will

I will walk the path God has directed for me.

I will shine brightly so others can see me miles away.

I will dedicate my life to my purpose.

I will guide others who are in need.

I will enlighten those who are unknowledgeable.

I will take each second, minute, and hour to praise my Father.

I will forever be grateful to Him.

My days are greater only because of God's promise. The moments spent with Him provide a solace that can't be explained. In times of doubt, my faithfulness comforts me. God has been clearing my path. I'm opening my soul to my Father. He has anointed my soul over and over again. Thank you, God, for having me by your side.

I will connect my spiritual life with leading a healthy life for my body. My body is the temple of the Holy Ghost. I will handle it with care.

I will not be a sacrificial lamb for anyone, especially those who envy me.

I will be open to the purpose that was created just for me.

I will live to enlighten and love the people that surround me.

I will be confident to stand in a room full of leaders.

I will only be the head and not the tail.

Self-Affirmations - Check-In

- 27 -

Do you recite self-affirmations every day? List five self-affirmations

Keep

Accepting

Righteousness

More

Abundantly

Is the only way.........

I am a part of God's tribe. I can conquer the most any enemy throws in my direction. I can and will demolish all the stones that once barricaded me. I shall walk in the light God has directed for me. To all those who challenge me, I shall not fear those fragmented thoughts that once shadowed me.

I am greater than my enemies who rise up against me. I am smarter than those who talk down about me. I am stronger than those that fight me. I have all of these qualities because of God's love.

I will only seek favor and acceptance from God. He matters most because He created me.

Look in the mirror and recite these three most powerful words in the universe daily: **I LOVE YOU!**

Self-Affirmations - Check-In

Are you embracing your inner strengths? List your inner strengths.

Am I For Sale?

Am I for sale? I will stop putting my feelings on clearance for people to hurt me. I should NEVER mark down my value! An experience with me will always be priceless.

I am God's child. He created me for His purpose. Today, tomorrow, and forever, I will only serve him.
- 32 -

I will be the solution, not the problem. I will walk in God's word. My spirit will not give in to the power trying to conquer me.

I am

- 33 -

I am love.

I am intelligent.

I am beautiful. I am great.

I am bold.

I am transparent.

I am thoughtful.

I am justified. I am a warrior.

I am a leader. I am a listener.

I am a rock.

I am a giver. I am a lover.

I am a Christian.

I am God's child. Guess what?

I am enough!

I am justifiably proud of all of my accomplishments.

I stand with God. He's my guiding force. No weapon formed against me shall prosper.

I am the light that will never dim. Today, I will shine brighter than yesterday.

I am genuine. I will not be blocked from my purpose.

I'm a witness to God's glory. He has placed me amongst people that will uplift me. No lack of discernment will ever block me.

I am talented, ambitious, and honorable. No one shall ever cast their doubts on me.

I am the moral compass that will help others sail through life.

I will be an invigorator for those that need my strength.

I will relax more to enjoy life. I do not want to worry about the "check engine" sign notifying me my body needs rest.

Today, I shall rise before those who want to hurt me.

I will not feel defeated.

I am an example of God's love. I will forever walk in His image.

I was spared by God's grace. In return, I will give grace to others.

I will accept constructive criticism to help shape my vision.

My ambitious spirit will always ask God for guidance.

I will always stand on the side of righteousness.

I am a leader, not a follower.

I will always consider the feelings of others.

I will expand my entrepreneurial brand.

Self-Affirmations - Check-In

Are you building a positive mindset?

List five positive characteristics you possess.

I will be ok with removing fake friends from my life.

I will only be accessible to those who allow me to enter their space, especially people who give their time to me and are transparent with me.

My life will never be filled with drama.

I shall only fill my soul with positive energy.

I will not take more financial responsibility.

I will articulate my feelings more often so I'm not misunderstood.

I am a diamond that will forever sparkle in the eyes of my soulmate.

I will always dance for love that was meant just for me.

I am standing on solid ground. Therefore, no one can knock me off my square.

I will not allow others to discourage me.

I am releasing the past to usher in my future.

I will replace negativity in my life, replenish my positive sides, and repeat inspirational words daily.

I will no longer be afraid of change.

I am excited to live in God's promise.

I am determined to overcome the fear of climbing to the top. I will succeed at climbing mountains that were once too steep for me to climb.

I will no longer sit on the sidelines of life. It is time for me to make the winning shot. Get ready, world, because I'm rebounding to my true self.

I am strong and capable of elevating myself to break any generational curse.

I am deleting the world's noise to focus on myself.

I will meet every challenge with a strong mind.

I will not allow distractions to compromise my time.

I will never give up.

I will no longer isolate myself from people who care about my well-being.

I am living a calm, free, and easy life. Interruptions are not allowed.

I will not be recycled. My love isn't bendable for people to toss in the recycle bin when they no longer need me.

I will no longer date emotionally broken people. They are banned from my life.

I am an original that can never be duplicated.

I will never use dependency as a crutch to maneuver through life. Gaining independence is the only way to survive adulthood.

I am dedicated to my peace of mind. I will not allow others to disrupt my life.

I will be ready for God to enlarge my territory.

I will always be the author of my story. No one will ever write my story better than me.

I am designed to walk in alignment with God's purpose.

I will always lead my life as Christ has required, with integrity.

I am the sun that will always rise to shine on others.

I am the gift that was created to restore calmness in people's lives.

I will not take life for granted. Each day is a gift beautifully wrapped in God's grace.

I wlll constantly evolve to a better version of myself.

I will lead with love, even with those that stand against me.

I will fulfill the purpose that was created for me.

I will create a network that will open doors for others.

I am priceless.

I will love and treat myself with respect.

I am designed to be loved.

I am more than the average girl. No one compares to me.

I will not compromise my beliefs.

I am the light that will never dim its shine, especially in the midst of my haters.

I will not be broken. My soul will not be stirred. I will forever stand in the love God has for me.

I will always bet on myself. It's hard trying to bet on others not knowing their true character.

I am the song with the sweetest melody that brings joy and peace in everyone's midst.

I am a game changer that will help my community succeed.

Love Notes

I am in control of my destiny.

I am the creator's child.

I will find happiness in myself before looking to others to provide it for me.

I am the present and the future. My life shall never be in the past tense.

I will delete every source of unhappiness from my life.

I will open the door God has made available for me to walk through.

I will never compromise my ability to inherit the territory that God has promised to me.

I will only seek refuge with God.

I will always honor and respect myself.

I am the bread and the butter.

I am the cream of the crop.

I am the painting that will forever be shown in the minds of those who want to see me.

I will always carry the top-flight spirit. God created me to soar.

I am the book written to be read only by people wanting to hear meaningful words.

I will heal my brokenness.

I will love my enemies.

I will perform to the best of my abilities in every assignment God has given me.

I will protect my family.

I will honor God.

I am an example of God's love.

Love Notes

I will work to correct my weaknesses.

I am a prayer warrior.

I am the voice of reason.

I am divinely crafted by God to be a wife.

I am divinely crafted by God to be a husband.

I am not a bitter person.

I will be a good mother.

I will be a good father.

I am a phoenix rising like the sun. I will rise above all.

I will change all the ugliness that resides in me.

I am not a failure. I will always learn from my mistakes.

I will be an obedient child.

I am walking with faith.

I am worthy to be loved.

I will turn self-hate into self-love.

I will love myself over and over again.

I am my husband's love note.

I am my wife's love melody.

I will give grace to others as God has done for me.

I will walk with confidence even when I have self-doubts.

I will press pause on negativity in my life.

I will become a better listener.

Love Notes

I am becoming the person God created for His will.

- 47 -

I will not grieve my past. I am only living in the present and looking towards the future God has constructed for me.

I am repairing my life from the shattered glass that once held me back from walking my path. Get ready, world! I will have a clear path to freedom. I will not walk through or walk over pieces of glass anymore.

Love Notes

I will no longer be disrespectful.

I will not allow my arrogance to self-destruct my journey. I will be humble, loving, giving, and caring to others.

I will not allow someone to dismantle my character.

I am the epitome of love.

Thrive to be an asset instead of a liability. Get healed!

I don't need validation.

I am not sorry. God's favor is all over me.

I will reduce stress by releasing people that cause my spirit to unhinge.

I am the sun, moon, and stars that have a distinct presence on this earth.

Self-Affirmations Notes

- 50 -

Ezra 10:4 "Rise up; this matter is in your hands.

We will support you, so take courage and do it."

Self-Affirmations Notes

Ezra 10:4 "Rise up; this matter is in your hands.

We will support you, so take courage and do it."

Self-Affirmations Notes

- 52 -

Ezra 10:4 "Rise up; this matter is in your hands.

We will support you, so take courage and do it."

CHAPTER 2

Spirituality

spirituality

noun

spir·i·tu·al·i·ty   ˌspir-i-chə-ˈwa-lə-tē

plural: spiritualities

a: something that in ecclesiastical law belongs to the church or to a cleric as such

b: CLERGY

c: sensitivity or attachment to religious values

d: the quality or state of being spiritual

Our spirituality connects to our spirit, mind, and soul, allowing us to breathe positive energy. Our connection to God often allows us to find peace within ourselves. My spiritual journey has humbled me over the years. God has carried me through many storms that could have taken me out. I take pride in knowing my walk with God was uniquely carved out for only me. My life story will change over and over again.

Let me tell you something that should be deposited inside of you. Your spirit, mind, soul, and breathing are required to survive. God gave us the blessing to have a spirit to submit to Him, a mind to think of Him, a soul to relinquish to Him, and breath to praise Him. These would not be given to us if God had not given His only son to save the world. When we accept Jesus Christ as our Lord and Savior, we are giving the Holy Spirit permission to enter our bodies to give us life that was ordained by God. We can confess to God in our native tongue all our desires without alerting the enemy.

Our minds are free from the travesties that once were formed from our unjust thinking. We are more knowledgeable and no longer bound by the worldly sins that once clouded our minds to think more openly and widely about our purpose.

Our souls are cleansed and pure to accept God's love through which we are able to love others, especially those who dislike us. Our souls are given immortality. That's a blessing. Our souls will forever live and rejoice in God's house. Our souls will be able to reconnect with family and friends that accepted God.

In John 14:6, Jesus said, "I am the way, and the truth, and the life. No one comes to the Father except through me." The moment we accept God, doors that once were closed will open.

Prayer for Spirituality

- 56 -

Father God, I come to you standing in the need of prayer. I'm praying for humility, kindness, admiration, and wisdom. You have continuously carried me through every storm. My life's status is all due to your outpouring love. You have wrapped your loving arms around me for my safety. I pray that you continue to enrich my life not with material items but with your love and many blessings. You know all my wants and needs. I humbly ask for all of your blessings to continue to support my life.

In Jesus' name. Amen

Seek Christ

Are you feeling down? You feel no one cares?

Seek Christ.

Do you feel lonely as you walk through your day?

Seek Christ.

Do you feel hurt over a broken relationship?

Seek Christ.

Do you feel anger that stems from disappointment?

Seek Christ.

Can you hear haters dispelling your calling?

Seek Christ.

Are you broken and require healing?

Seek Christ.

As you can see, the only one that can help you in any situation is Christ. Reach out to him. Call His name to heal and fix your needs. Double down, stand on God's word, and hear His voice. He will speak to you.

Just seek Christ.

My former self was tested and laid to rest. I was held down by complacent thinking. But great is my Lord. He gave me strength. I am victorious over all my obstacles. I will rise like the phoenix bird untouched. I will resurrect into the person God created for His purpose.

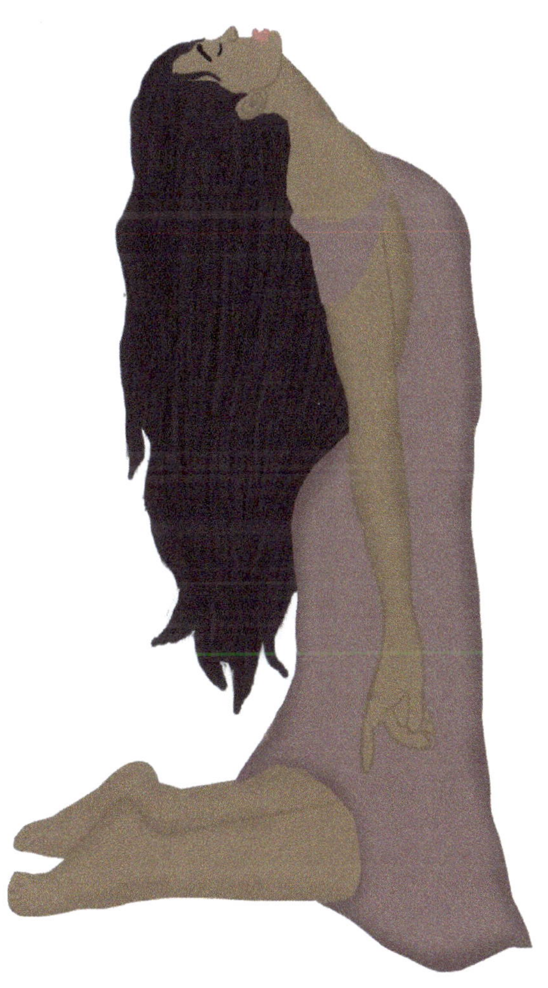

"Love your enemies as you love yourself. Show them love will overthrow any darkness that tries to dim your light."

Imagine

Imagine a world full of love. The skies are filled with refreshing air. There's no hate from anywhere. People are bubbling with joy. There are no more devils that can destroy. You're easily gliding through life, always praising Jesus Christ. He saw this day from the beginning. Look y'all, everyone is winning. Not a day goes by without thanking God because He is wise. He knows us all. God wiped away all our fears. Now, there are no more tears. Imagine that there is no way to fail. You're loving this new life with major appeal. I can't complain about the past. Those days were erased fast. Imagine a world with a love that will last forever.

God's Presence

God spoke to me with a strong voice. It was calm and soothing to hear. I felt His presence as I looked around the room. I knew my Father was near. He gave me instructions. His whisper was so clear. I honored His wish. I had good news that would bring someone cheer. I was an intercessor to confirm the person's prayers were heard. He saw her weeping, asking for His help. He caught her tears with His love. Her prayers and cries didn't go unnoticed. God selected me to provide the news of saving grace. I'm so thankful He called me to this place. I want to feel God's presence again. Lord, please use me because I love to hear God's voice that's softer than the wind.

Alone

What does it mean to be alone?

Absolutely nothing because you are surrounded by God.

Amazing Times

Once, there was a time when I cried due to unhappiness in my life, but I was reminded of all of those amazing times life allowed me to love, grow, and conquer. God wrapped me up in His love. He was determined never to let go of my hand.

Laughter has filled my life with a brightness that shines like the sun. Feeling joy is an amazing time. I now cry tears of joy that no longer have stains of sorrow. My life has changed for the good. God has provided me with forever amazing times.

"Compassion is the best way to give to those who are less fortunate. But compassion must start with you. Granted, this is new for me. It wouldn't be possible without Jesus, who died for me."

A Race to Seek Christ

During the pandemic, I thought about my relationship with God. I was always thinking my relationship should be stronger. I prayed and always thanked God for His blessings. The coronavirus had me thinking about me and my kids' salvation. I constantly thought about my kids' relationship with Jesus Christ. I prayed for their relationship with Jesus. I do not want them to feel the wrath of God. However, I feel it might be too late. I believe the world is experiencing this plague because of our refusal to repent. We are not building a relationship with God because it's not a priority.

2 Chronicles 7:14 says, "If my people, who are called by my name, will humble themselves and pray and seek my face and turn from their wicked ways, then I will hear from heaven, and I will forgive their sin and will heal their land." We were warned that at the name of Jesus, every knee will bow, and every living thing will confess the name of God. Scriptures has given us a roadmap to our Father, an urgency to confess and repent our sins. People, wake up your slumbering souls. We are in a race to seek Christ. Start praying and thanking God for His blessings. He wants recognition for His work. Work

diligently on family members who are lost. Give them the tools to jump every hurdle and sprint to the finish line with Christ.

Words cannot describe the way I am so grateful to God. He's blessing me in the midst of this storm. I'm thankful for God's covering. I will always call His name. There's no wavering from him. I trust His path for me. I'm standing on His word FOREVER

Pain Will Produce Your Promise

Everyone will experience pain in their life. Pain is a part of our reality. There is no way around it. I've experienced the most pain losing someone. Whether it was through death, break-ups, or just ghosting, be real with yourself. Dig deep to tap into that pain. You will be frustrated with the process. No matter the depth of your pain, trust that it will produce your promise.

"How to win a losing game? Trust God!"

"Rise up, king. You can depend on God. Your destiny was created to lead, protect, and provide for your family. Better days will follow shortly. Don't let superficial beginnings determine your path. Focus on your crown. Don't give up. You got this!"

Sadness

Moments of sadness are filled with emptiness. Emotions are dreary and cold. I can't shake the darkness that has overshadowed my light. Standing in the midst of my storm, I feel heaviness. My thoughts of light slowly left me. But God! God has sent the Holy Spirit to redeem me. My faithfulness in God has shifted my dark moments to light. I feel my soul become renewed. I can boldly breathe in the love of God.

Spirituality - Check-In

Are you connected with God? If no, explain why.

If yes, describe your connection.

____

____

____

____

____

____

____

____

____

Dirty

Flowing from my heart I have a stream of tears. I felt God's presence over the years. He has embraced my soul. Now, it's time for the true me to unfold. He gathered me up from the floor. I was so dirty, but that's no more. I've wept several times because I finally realized the Heavenly Father is all mine.

Life

Life is given to us as a gift. We breathe the air our creator, the Almighty God, made for us. Our eyes see the beautiful earth. God holds us accountable for the image we show. Wielding to sin, we find fault in others. We should look deeply at ourselves because hurting others only illustrates the evil that sees no end but death. Focus on being an exemplary Christian. Walk in God's light so others can follow. Stride and walk in the presence of God. Know your truth lies in God's bosom. Living for everlasting life brings peace over the extremities of the world. Constantly pray for the lives of others, not forgetting those who rise up against you. God has provided you with knowledge of all things, good and bad. Demonstrate to others your life has a calling from God. Don't be afraid to be the source to show His light. You've only begun His journey. Now take this flight.

"You got this! Don't walk away scared to face your trauma. Grab it, deal with it, and make peace with it. It's the only way your soul will stop unraveling."

"Listen to God's divine instruction to complete your task. God has given all of us assignments that will provide assistance to others."

Spirituality - Check-In

Have you found inner peace? If so, describe the feeling.

Pain

Taking notes of this extreme pain, I never want to feel it again. Knowing that love is loss keeps tugging at my heart. I'm amazed that I haven't fallen apart. My life has shifted for good. I never thought I could or would move past the agony I felt. But I've been praying, asking God to move me on the path of His will. He's taken my hand, gently guiding me through this pain, navigating my steps to remain sane. As the days went by, the pain I felt was erased, along with my tears. I thank God for His presence through the years. Leaning on my Father will forever last. I'm just thankful He's forgiven me for my past.

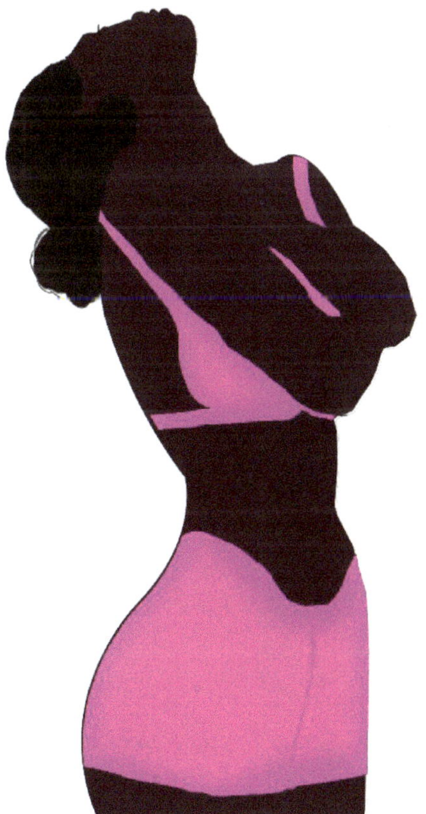

"Faithfulness is required to have a close relationship with God. God has provided us with many blessings. God has continuously rescued us from unbearable situations that have traumatized our well-being. He has pulled us in His bosom for protection. How can we complain about God? We can't because my God is always on time. He may not come when you want Him. He comes when we are ready to receive His presence."

Spirituality - Check~In

Have you explored your spiritual path? If so, describe your
journey

____

____

____

____

____

____

____

____

Spirituality Notes

- 72 -

Deuteronomy 7:9 "Know therefore that the LORD your God is God; he is the faithful God, keeping His covenant of love to a thousand generations of those who love him and keep His commandments."

Spirituality Notes

Deuteronomy 7:9 "Know therefore that the LORD your God is God; he is the faithful God, keeping His covenant of love to a thousand generations of those who love him and keep His commandments."

Spirituality Notes

- 74 -

Deuteronomy 7:9 "Know therefore that the LORD your God is God; he is the faithful God, keeping His covenant of love to a thousand generations of those who love him and keep His commandments."

CHAPTER 3

Relationships

Relationship

noun

re·la·tion·ship   ri-ˈlā-shən-ˌship

1 : the state of being <u>related</u> or interrelated

studied the relationship between the variables

2 : the <u>relation</u> connecting or binding participants in a relationship: such as

A : <u>KINSHIP</u>

B : a specific instance or type of kinship

3 a: a state of affairs existing between those having <u>relations</u> or dealings

b: a romantic or passionate attachment

Relationships can be hard sometimes, especially when people are experiencing pain that was never resolved. We can bring our own pain into relationships with the mindset that it's either us or them. This attitude stems from not trusting others based on past experiences. 1 Corinthians 13:4-7 states, "Love is patient, love is kind. It does not envy, it does not boast, it is not proud. 5 It does not dishonor others, it is not self-seeking, it is not easily angered, it keeps no record of wrongs. 6 Love does not delight in evil but rejoices with the truth. 7 It always protects, always trusts, always hopes, always perseveres."

Good relationships are always treasured. I've gained and lost relationships over the years. I truly believe everyone has a season to contribute to your life. However, we need to decipher when their season has ended. This has been hard for me. I've severed ties with people that were like my family. I have opined for many years on where things went wrong. I prayed about my decision. God gave me the direction and the approval. It's okay to love people from a distance.

Prayer for Relationships

- 77 -

Heavenly Father, I thank you for all the relationships that I've experienced in my life. Every relationship has taught me that respect, patience, and kindness are required to have key connections to others. I thank you for weaving out people that were not good for me. I thank you for not allowing my heart to harden due to strenuous connections to others. Thank you for bringing people into my life to open doors that would have been shut. Thank you for bringing people into my life who truly love me for my authenticity. Thank you for providing me with a family that truly cares about my well-being. But most of all, thank you for my relationship with you.

You have been my Alpha and Omega through it all. In Jesus' name, Amen

"I've met some phenomenal people. I never knew their purpose or contribution to my life until God was ready for me to understand their value. People have silently watched me over the years. I've been given opportunities due to my character and hard work. God will lead strangers into our lives to open doors that would have been closed to us. Building relationships with people with the same morals and beliefs is imperative to find opportunities. Don't be afraid to start new relationships. Trust God to lead you to the right people that can enhance your life. Life-changing opportunities mostly occur when you are connected to the right people."

"Step out in faith to meet exceptional people and build everlasting relationships."

Peace

When seeking peace, start within yourself. Sometimes, there are fragments in our lives that should be woven together. We live our lives in broken relationships that interfere with our happiness. We must repair our spirits before peace can be found in our atmosphere. Our minds must be stripped of all the negativity that surrounds us. There's a certain calmness that falls on our naked souls because once we are cleansed, our minds feel a new beginning. It's time. Don't let peace leave you behind. Walk with peace and enjoy life!

Relationships - Check-In

Do you have relationship challenges? Identify your challenging relationships. Describe those challenges.

____

____

____

____

____

____

____

____

Mask

I change my mask every day. Each mask tells my story for the day. I wear a mask to shield my pain because people would say I'm insane. I guard my feelings within, always wishing that bad events in my life wouldn't happen again. I've experienced so much heartache in my life. I don't know how I handled so much strife. I have several masks that help me cope with my lost hope. I'm tired of wearing a mask. I pray that the circumstances in my life change fast. I have called out to God many times before I put on a mask. I hope God sees my tears behind this closet door. I'm praying to God that I never need a mask. That life will be no more.

Suddenly, light appears. It shows me how to cope with my biggest fear. I've always wanted to experience love. I never was once hugged. My mom and dad turned away. But that shining light was Grandma. She came to save the day. I'm finally in a safe and loving place. I can finally put away those masks. My family and friends can see my face at last.

"Keep shining and staying positive. We are not perfect, but we are perfect enough for God to love us. We sometimes sit clueless, trying to determine what happens. Sometimes, our soul weeps for understanding. I've had those moments. But God has stood in the empty space that was left by others. He's spoken to me and said, "Continue to be you," because we are not perfect, but perfect for God to love us."

"Broken people always leave others in broken pieces."

"I don't care how many relationships you enter to find happiness or search for someone like me. It will never work because there is only one genuine certified me. All others are imperfect to my worth."

"Similarities aren't the same as the original. Recognize someone's worth early."

Stage Play

Toleration will no longer be my norm. If I see you exhibit behavior that hinders my well-being, I'm exiting the stage door immediately because drama isn't my stage play.

"Stop pouring into people that do not pour into you. Do not give the same energy because that's exhausting. Just walk away for your sanity."

"I'm tired of pouring into people that suck the life out of me. Please give me some space. You've been so selfish. But I've always given you grace. I'm depleted in more ways than one. I can't pour anything more because that would be just dumb. Move out of the way. I have no more oil to pour into you today."

Squatters

Stop allowing people to become squatters in your head. Stop thinking about people who wronged you. Let them go. Move them out immediately. You need to get ready for that qualified buyer. They are ready to pay to live in your life. They are ready to give you their time, love, assistance, patience, and attention. It's time to evict those squatters for good!

"Don't base your self-worth on who you don't have. You are the best. Your self-worth isn't questionable. Pull yourself together, smile, and repeat to yourself, "I am worth everything to me."

"Learn how to ride out when a season has ended for a relationship. Never look Back."

"Never overcompensate in a relationship because some people will take advantage."

"Most of us would love to have meaningful relationships. The drive to have strong connections with people sometimes is the center of our life. We must remember to seek a meaningful relationship with God before constructing a relationship with others. God is the driving force in our life. He requires and demands our time with him. We must honor him first."

Relationships - Check-In

Are you able to build strong bonds with people you love?
Describe your journey.

____

____

____

____

____

____

____

____

____

Stay Mad

My way of life has been shaken. I never thought I would have fair weather friends. Why would you consistently stay in my presence? Deep down behind that smile, you've been hating on my essence. You used words to break me. Stay mad. I can speak my mind and finally be free. Are you surprised I rose through the fire? I'm laughing because you didn't kill my desire. Your words didn't discourage me. You wanted me to break into pieces so everyone could see. I think you are afraid of my elevation. Just wait until God has uncovered His plan for me. Get ready because I will continue to be in God's grace. Stay mad because my destination is coming soon. Where he's taking me, you won't ever see this place. You chastise me for the way that I am. Our so-called friendship was really a sham. I gave until I couldn't give no more. I finally realize we need to close this so-called friendship door. Stay mad and ride on the passenger side while I drive through life. Let go of your ego and work for more. A good job or a good man won't come knocking at your door. Stay mad at my race. That's why you will never be in first place.

Damaged Goods

Who walks around, leaving a trail of people behind hurt, confused, and devastated because they were charmed and fed lies? A damaged person is who. I never really understood the complexity of dating a damaged person. There are reasons people are attracted to damaged people. They appear to be loving, sweet, and considerate. People are drawn to them. They have all the qualities that made your checklist. There's a side of them unknown to others. Damage people will eat you up and spit you out on the side of the road. You would never see this coming. I call this person damaged goods. They will blindside you without flinching. A damaged person is hurting as they continue to bleed all over others who loved them. Essentially, it is never smart to date a damaged person. You will walk away feeling betrayed by the relationship. However, you will also have a love lesson from the experience. You should realize there is no way to change a damaged person. You cannot use ultimatums, scare tactics, or any other form of coercion. The choice to change must be their decision. They need that Aha moment to see their damage. They must work on themselves to heal for successful relationships in the future.

Sometimes, our heart desires someone so badly that we forget that our love journey should first start with God. If we focus on our relationship with God, a damaged person cannot enter our space. We would spot a damaged person right away. I've been in relationships with damaged people. Both relationships did not end well for me. Those relationships taught me a valuable lesson. The last relationship showed me that I have the ability to love again. I shielded my heart for years after my divorce, fearing my heart would be torn into pieces again. I was able to gather pieces of my heart to glue each piece together. The process made me whole again.

Currently, I'm focusing on my relationship with God. My single season has been a journey. There have been times when I did not recognize myself. My single season has me pulling all of my layers off. I can finally see my trueness. I found my way to becoming close to God. I know there is someone that was created just for me. I can't wait to meet my life partner. I will be waiting patiently to avoid damaged goods.

"I'm junk in your eyes, but I will be a treasure to another person who has undying love for me. You do not define who I am. Your disdain for me means nothing. I do not care. You are irrelevant."

Relationships - Check-In

Have you embraced your vulnerability? Please explain.

____

____

____

____

____

____

____

____

____

I Owe You Many Thanks

Thank you for removing me from your rotation.

Thank you for stop calling me.

Thank you for not spending time with me.

Thank you for lying to me.

Thank you for cheating on me.

Thank you for abandoning me.

Thank you for not loving me

Thank you for trying to tear me down.

Thank you for gossiping about me.

Thank you for not valuing me.

Thank you for being jealous of me.

Thank you for not leaving your wife.

Thank you for not leaving your husband.

Thank you for blindly missing my worth.

Thank you for misleading me.

Thank you for abusing me.

Thank you for giving me a STD.

Thank you for using me for my money.

Thank you for using me for a meal.

Thank you for gaslighting me.

Thank you for finally ditching your representative. I finally see the real you. You made it easier for me to walk away. For all, most, some, or even just one of these actions against me, I owe you many thanks for being just as you are in this world.

Relationship Notes

- 94 -

1 Corinthians 13:4-7 "Love is patient, love is kind. It does not envy, it does not boast, it is not proud. 5 It does not dishonor others, it is not self-seeking, it is not easily angered, it keeps no record of wrongs. 6 Love does not delight in evil but rejoices with the truth. 7 It always protects, always trusts, always hopes, always perseveres."

Relationship Notes

- 95 -

1 Corinthians 13:4-7 "Love is patient, love is kind. It does not envy, it does not boast, it is not proud. 5 It does not dishonor others, it is not self-seeking, it is not easily angered, it keeps no record of wrongs. 6 Love does not delight in evil but rejoices with the truth. 7 It always protects, always trusts, always hopes, always perseveres."

Relationship Notes

1 Corinthians 13:4-7 "Love is patient, love is kind. It does not envy, it does not boast, it is not proud. 5 It does not dishonor others, it is not self-seeking, it is not easily angered, it keeps no record of wrongs. 6 Love does not delight in evil but rejoices with the truth. 7 It always protects, always trusts, always hopes, always perseveres."

CHAPTER 4

Grief

Grief

noun ˈgrēf

a : deep and poignant distress caused by or as if by bereavement his grief over his son's death

b : a cause of such suffering life's joys and griefs

Grief can leave you stuck in a place that has your spirit wrapped in so much pain. People can grieve the death of a relationship, which is rarely talked about in society, and the death of a loved one. I remember my first experience of feeling grief. I felt sharp pains in my stomach. I could not eat anything. My body was numb. I could not feel anything when my maternal grandfather said my maternal grandmother had died. I was seven years old when she died. She was my everything. I could not believe she was no longer with us. Reality struck when I saw her lying in the casket. It was unbearable for me to see her in that state. I remember having an out-of-body experience walking towards the casket to view her body. I screamed in agony, with tears flowing so fast. I did not know how to process her death. No one asked if I was ok. No one explained to me that my grandmother's passing would not be the last experience with death. I was young, clueless, and scared to understand death would always be a part of my life. A couple of years later, my maternal grandfather died. That was when I realized death was not going anywhere. Death is a part of life. No one has the luxury of living on earth forever. Death is a natural order for all living things.

During my divorce, both of my paternal grandparents died suddenly. I was in a tailspin trying to figure out how to handle these emotions. I felt this was definitely a test from God. This grieving process was so different because I was grieving the death of a relationship with my husband and my grandparents. My grandfather died before my grandmother. He had a massive heart attack while working. Walking into the emergency room and seeing him living only because of machines was devasting. At that moment, I knew my grandaddy was no longer there. My grandmother passed away a few months later. I adored my grandparents. It was pure heartbreak to no longer talk or laugh with them. I just remember asking God for covering. I was crushed. My grandparents were gone. Matthew 5:4 states, "Blessed are those who mourn, for they shall be comforted." God has always been my source of strength during times of bereavement. I find solace in knowing that my loved ones and I will meet again.

It is hard to grasp that I just saw or spoke with someone, and then in the blink of an eye, they are gone forever. I have learned to lean on God to usher me through my grieving process. When one of my best friends died suddenly, I called her cell phone just to hear her voice. After her death, it took me years to understand tomorrow is not guaranteed. However, God has promised us eternal life when we accept Him as our Lord and Savior. No one will live forever.

We are here only for a certain time. It is important to love each other while there is still breath in our bodies. Our death date is unknown until it's time for us to return to God.

The grieving process for the death of a loved one or relationship is the same. There are five stages of grief that people will encounter in processing the loss. The first stage of the grieving process is denial. Denial has a delayed response for the person to accept the loss. Accepting the loss recognizes the reality the loss has occurred in their life. The second stage in the grieving process is anger. Anger is the emotion that occurs when the reality of loss has finally set in the person's life. The pain felt during a loss can be unbearable. The question "Why did this happen?" will play over and over in someone's mind. The third stage in the grieving process is bargaining. Bargaining is used to rationalize the loss. People often turn to God in this phase, making a deal wishing to change the reality of the loss. The fourth stage in the grieving process is depression. Depression occurs during this stage because the death of a loved one or relationship is a new reality that is not easy to accept. It is painful to continue life without the person you love. When people cannot move forward, a therapist is required to provide coping mechanisms to get out of depression. The final stage of the grieving process is acceptance. Finally, accepting the loss does not relieve the pain. It only allows the person to come to terms with the new norm. Time will allow a person to process the loss and move forward. Everyone will experience the grieving process. No one can escape grief. Can you imagine the pain Mary felt seeing her son dying on the cross? She trusted God in that moment of grieving her son. Psalms 34:18 says, "The Lord is near to the brokenhearted and saves the crushed in spirit." Always trust God during your grieving process.

Prayer for Grief

Father, I will continually praise your name. I have a tremendous pain that is piercing my heart. I look to you for healing and resolve. Father, I cry out to you because your promise will forever comfort me. I shall cherish the memories that were shared. I need you right now to lift me. I have a heavy sorrow that's intense over my soul. I pray that this too shall pass. I pray for strength and peace to endure this loss. Comfort me, oh Lord.

In Jesus' name. Amen

Grief - Check-In

How do you handle grief? Describe your coping mechanism(s) for dealing with grief.

____

____

____

____

____

____

____

____

____

Grief

Grief is an indescribable pain that shakes you. It stirs your core. If not checked, the pain will consume you. Pour beautiful memories that were once shared in your soul. Remember, cherishing their life is the only goal. Don't let grief continue to have a hold on your life. Let go of this sharp pain that has reshaped your heart. Your loved one will always be a part of you. Release them from this mortal form. God has covered their spirit. They will forever live with you. Find comfort knowing their spirit is now sitting next to God on His throne.

Gentle God

Gently, God has taken my hand. He is leading me to the Promised Land. I hear the trumpets roar, and now I realize my pain is no more. As I walk closer to heaven's door, I see Momma waiting to greet me. She's standing there with her arms stretched, waiting to comfort me. I'm so delighted to see my family that has passed. We are celebrating my homecoming at last. I'm finally home. God has let me in. I'm safe and have reunited with my family again. Don't cry for me because I'm healed. No more pain I shall feel. Until we meet again, I will be in heaven waiting, rejoicing with God's angels.

Angels Gathering at My Feet

As angels gather at my feet, I feel the covering God has bestowed upon me. As I walk through life, I can feel God guiding my path. He's there to hold my hand in my time of need. He's my strength when I feel weak. He has angels gathering at my feet to watch over me. God commanded each angel to watch over me so I can overcome all the evil that comes after me only to kill my will. God is my protector with His angels that gather at my feet. No man or evil spirit can defeat me because my God oversees my life as angels gather at my feet.

"Living life as God saw fit is the best. I can see life through His eyes. I'm so thankful for the times shared with loved ones. Reminiscing on times that past, enjoying life as if it's my last. The leaves are blowing as trees sit still. I'm so thankful that God has given me His will."

Grief - Check-In

Are you able to honor memories of your love ones? List the most beautiful memories you have to treasure.

____

____

____

____

____

____

____

____

____

Glories of Heaven

Time heals all pain, but this devastating loss and emptiness I feel will undoubtedly remain. I think of all the conversations we had talking about the joys of life. We also talked about those things and people that caused us strife. No time to dwell on the past. You may be gone, but this sisterhood will last forever. I'm no longer worried about your pain. You've been picked up by the glories of heaven that calmly whispered your name. I can hear the sound of heaven's gates opening for you. You anticipate seeing God holding out His arms to you. You are excited as the glories of heaven whisk you through. You have finally gained your space among those who never wavered from God's grace. Glories of heaven never make a mistake. God sends His angels for those waiting to touch His hand. Glories of heaven call each name as God commands. We are destined by God to hear our name called by the glories of heaven.

Grief - Check-In

- 107 -

Have you transformed your pain into your purpose?

Provide insight into your transformation.

____

____

____

____

____

____

____

____

____

Connections Lost

Grieving someone's transition almost feels like a disconnection. Their voice, touch, smell, and presence are no longer near you. You are unable to connect physically. However, remembering times spent with the person no longer here will reconnect you in your heart. The pain will always be there. But the love you have for them will outweigh the pain you feel. You will carry that love until your connection is lost when you return to our God.

Grief Notes

Psalms 34:18 "The LORD is close to the brokenhearted and saves those who are crushed in spirit."

Grief Notes

Psalms 34:18 "The LORD is close to the brokenhearted and saves those who are crushed in spirit."

____

____

____

____

____

____

____

____

____

Grief Notes

Psalms 34:18 "The LORD is close to the brokenhearted and saves those who are crushed in spirit."

____

____

____

____

____

____

____

____

____

CHAPTER 5

Motivaton

motivation

noun / ˌmōdəˈvāSH(ə)n/

a: the act or process of motivating

Some students need motivation to help them through school.

b: the condition of being motivated employees who lack motivation

c: a motivating force, stimulus, or influence : INCENTIVE, DRIVE

Oh boy, motivation is quite the topic to talk about with you. Motivation is the key to achieving dreams that were crafted just for you. There were plenty of times when I just felt drained. I could not gather my thoughts to write a single sentence. I needed something to motivate me.

Procrastination crept in like a thief in the night. Finally, I realized fear was holding me back. Proverbs 20:4 states, "The sluggard does not plow in the autumn; he will seek at harvest and have nothing." I allowed fear to outweigh my passion to pursue my purpose. The more you lack motivation and procrastinate to accomplish any goal, the longer you delay the journey etched for you by God. Do not let your purpose lie on the shelf, gathering dust. You are required to complete the task that was given by God. For many years, I walked the earth without thinking about my purpose. It was only after I endured pain that my walk began to become closer to God. Surrendering to God's purpose became my motivation. My thoughts were focused on the steps required to complete my journey.

Prayer for Motivation

I am standing in the need of prayer for motivation. I find myself unable to move forward because of procrastination or fear of failure. Guide me to the path that was constructed for me. Speak life over my endeavor to give me ideas to pursue your destiny. I want to be your servant who provides light and love to others. Help me move through every mountain and storm that may block my view. Give me the courage and knowledge to move forward with your plan. I declare and decree that I will not be bound but free to continue my purpose. I am asking you humbly to motivate my spirit to move in your light.

Amen

Fearless

Fearless, we rise to any occasion. We chase our dreams and remember that the gifts bestowed on us by God are for us. We live, thrive, and remain a driven force in the lives of others because God appointed us to be fearless leaders. I will not dominate you. My gift is to guide you on this journey given to you. Trust your faith and move forward. There are so many plans to execute. There is no time to sit and think of the what-ifs. We can do it.

Motivation - Check-In

- 115 -

Are you fueling your passion? List your goals.

Create a plan to achieve each goal.

____

____

____

____

____

____

____

____

____

Peach Tree

You can be THEE sweetest peach on the tree, but you will always have that one peach that ain't ripe. It will do anything to be THEE sweetest peach. Its bitterness will turn to branches to shake you. But you are THEE sweetest peach on the tree. You have strong ties to your branch. I don't care how many times you are hit. You will never be released from that tree until your own branch says it's time to be free!

Favor Ain't Fair

- 117 -

Favor ain't fair for those that want your gift. Your crown is shining so bright your haters are plotting a rift. Don't worry about them. You were created to serve God. He will protect you from the hate. Remember to serve God because He knows your fate.

"I'm convinced your soul dies when dreams do not come to fruition."

Motivation - Check-In

Are you a procrastinator? List your obstacles.

____

____

____

____

____

____

____

____

____

Broken Dreams

My days, nights, hours, and seconds seem to melt together. I have no sense of time. My mind is racing to a destination that never appears. My fears have overcome my dreams for my near future. I can never complete a task; it seems my dreams are drifting away fast. I've been in this place too many times. I try to come to a certain space that would allow me to bear all of this weight. I cannot think of anything that would last. I thought these broken dreams would come to pass. I wait and wait to come together, but my dreams seem to be placed in a box called "Never". Subconsciously, I feel like a hair split in two because I'm divided on what to do. I think of other dreams to come, but it's never enough, which is just dumb. I've fallen into a most difficult place. My attitude is such a disgrace. I'm embarrassed because my momma didn't raise me this way. My tears stain my pillow every night because my dreams will never see daylight.

You see, I'm sleeping forever. My broken dreams have eternally been severed.

Chasing a Dream

Living life day to day, I have dreams of becoming the greatest of something. Right now, I can't say. I remember living in my dreams being the best something, but I can't remember most parts of the dream. I sit back and visualize being something supreme. Damn, if I can only remember what was in that dream. I'm passionate about becoming so many things. I can't pinpoint anything unless it was in my dream. Living life to the fullest is the best. I hope my days become clearer because I'm tired of chasing my dream.

Setbacks

Don't worry about any setbacks you've experienced. There's always that step up that will be 10 times more than that setback. Keep pushing. Never give up!

"Don't let the world dictate your path. Every negative comment towards your goal was created to defeat your purpose. Start believing in yourself to conquer all the self-doubt you are feeling. You are a soldier. Come out fighting for your purpose."

"When God opens the door, I'm running, not walking through. He knows my heart's desire. It's mine."

"Vision without work is dead! Don't let laziness or procrastination kill your purpose."

Finding Your Purpose

What's your passion?

What do you like to do in your spare time? What motivates you?

Do you have aspirations?

Do you listen to your inner voice?

Ask these questions to determine your purpose.

"Haters will hate me because of my blessings. I don't care about their misplaced feelings. I have God's favor. Staying in my Father's light is my only concern."

"Wake up fierce to take on the world."

"Take a breath and exhale all the issues that have overwhelmed you. If you don't, those issues will consume every breath you take. It will define your mood for the day, so just breathe and exhale all that concerns you out of the way."

Be Your Peace

Be your peace. Don't let people defeat you.

Sometimes, the attacks are meant for you. It's just a test.

You need to be tough so your attacker knows you've had enough. Don't walk away scared because there's a breakthrough just for you.

Be your peace so people can see your resiliency. Grab your peace; don't let haters shift it. Take your peace back. You can win this fight. Remember, be your peace; it's only right.

"Don't worry about the wall before you. Concern yourself with the brick to build the Wall."

Beauty Arise

Beauty arise, beauty arise. Cuz you are the gift to all eyes. Your charm can sway anyone to give in to your way. Your smile beams through any shade. Those who hate you know you've got it made. Keep shining, girl. Your kindness has made this your world.

"Hello, beautiful... remember you were eloquently made by God. You are the gift crafted to multiply everything you touch. Go make greatness today."

"Hello, handsome. Remember God constructed you to be a leader. He handcrafted you specifically first to run the world!"

"You shall rise to every occasion most times, but with God, it will happen all the time. Doors will fly open for you just when you thought I could never go through. Make your way from the past. Your somber days will not last. Keep your thoughts pure. You will feel God's love. His guidance will make you feel secure. Go conquer the world because it's yours, that's for sure."

"Live, love, and layer up in God's blessings today!"

Motivation - Check-In

Do you have a fire burning within that is pushing you forward?

Describe the feeling.

My Child...

My child, plant your feet on solid ground. I stand in prayer to the almighty God that your soul will never be bound. Look up high in the stratosphere; you have a calling on your life that every man shall fear. You are the strongest among us all. Keep striving to the top because, with God's guidance, you will never fall. Carry the gratitude that was embedded in your heart.

Remember you were blessed from the very start. Gather your tools to succeed. You are on your way to lead. Stand tall because you are the one that God has scheduled to rise like the sun; this journey you are on, no one has ever done!

"Take time to think about your future. You've waited too long. Your thoughts and ideas are almost gone. Remember, time moves faster than you can see. Sit down and decide what it's going to be."

"If you can't get a seat at the table, make a table for yourself and invite others to sit with you!"

"Be fierce, be extravagant, but most of all, be bold to get what's yours!"

"Stop walking through life, refusing to learn new things. If you continue, be okay with mediocrity."

"Be the force that can diminish any obstacle that is obstructing your view of success. Think of the grandest goal, then work towards achieving it. You hold the insight to developing ideas that were given to you. Strategize, prioritize, memorize, and realize you hold the keys to your success."

My Black Prince Shall Rise...

In the midst of being held back because of his skin, that experience won't shake him within. He knows racism will never win. He will remain Black and proud over and over again. He knows his birthright that was taught when his life began. My Black Prince Shall Rise... When he is denied a job because his qualification is not enough, he won't just sit back and accept someone's opinion. He will receive the experience and knowledge needed to advance ahead. This young man has the ability to run any company. He's just that tough.

My Black Prince Shall Rise...

At times of depression, he is pressed to feel down. He can hardly get dressed because of the open wound he feels bound. Time passed by that made him cry.

Determined to breathe in relief, he pulls out of this rabbit hole because he doesn't want to die. He will slay his current state of mind, standing on his faith.

My Black Prince Shall Rise...

During traumatic situations that occurred in his life, to release this pain, he yells out twice. He is strong to seek help. He knows it's time because of this agony he's never felt.

My Black Prince Shall Rise...

After he thinks the world has fallen on his shoulders, no one can understand the heaviness he is holding. He will put in the work to release this stress. The world is always putting him through some test.

My Black Prince Shall Rise...

As the police are harassing him without a reason, he realizes this is the season. This young man is keeping his composure, answering all questions with excellent responses that show his intelligence. No one can deny his integrity, brainpower, education, and personality are his prize.

My Black Prince Shall Rise...

Young Black boys are walking through life trying to determine their path. For some, it's a daunting task to create a map for their life. It's especially hard when good men are not represented in their lives. How can he create a map for his life to be a good man and contribute to society? He will know his worth to build his confidence. He will seek education to elevate his socioeconomic status. He will seek a mentor to teach him the responsibility and actions required to be a man when a male is not represented in his home. He will be an attribute to society. He will work for excellence to show the world.

My Black Prince Shall Rise...

"Your season is for a reason. God is there watching and guiding you through your hard season. He has not forgotten you. God will show you that His promise is still over you."

"Shortcomings are only temporary. Work on creating a plan to eliminate every drawback. Once you've completed this task, your elevation in life will go beyond your imagination."

"I won't get ready but stay ready. I know when the time is right, God will make it happen."

"God may be holding up your purpose because there will be a clearing in your life. Once those boulders are removed, you will have what God promised for you. Servants of God will always be rewarded."

You Are...

Unbreakable,

Unstoppable,

Unbendable,

Unshameable,

Undefiable,

Don't let the naysayers stop you from being phenomenal.

"You are not basic or average. There is NOTHING simplistic about you. You should never allow someone to validate your worth. You were created in God's image, not theirs. Pull yourself together. Acknowledge your worth. You are an exemplary person who has an assignment. You were created to be the gift that will forever be presented to others."

It's Your Winning Season!

Are you feeling depleted? Do you want to give up because life has thrown you too many curveballs? Wait. Please listen to my directive for you to enter your winning season. I do not care about your status, color, gender, or creed. Everyone deserves a winning season. There is a test called life. Let me tell you that "adulting" has its moments of uncertainty. I can count on all my fingers and toes, plus more, when the spirit of defeat tried to tear me down. There were times when I would smile on the outside with my soul crying on the inside. I wanted my life to exist without any obstacles. The nerve to think life should be perfect. I've learned from every test that obstacles were constructed to make you stronger. Growth only occurs when there are life-changing events. How could we navigate through life not knowing ways to pass tests that could diminish our faith, confidence, peace, and spirit?

Our path to completing our purpose depends on passing every test. There will always be moments that distract us from God's purpose. We cannot allow the enemy to interfere with our destiny. You must stand firm on the foundation that God uniquely created for you. I have been attacked so many times physically, mentally, financially, and spiritually. My only saving grace was relying on my foundation. My favorite scripture that reminds me of God's covering is Psalms 91:2: "He is my refuge and my fortress, my God, in whom I trust." This scripture reaffirms that God will always be our shield. Our faith is linked to trusting Him. We cannot have one without the other. We were marked for greatness before conception. Our achievements do not happen by chance, only by God's commission that provided the opportunity. We must work on pursuing our purpose.

First, ask God to reveal your purpose. Pray with an open heart to free your mind of any insecurities that would delay your acceptance. I want to warn you that you must be ready for the assignment. God is purposeful. He knows our strengths and weaknesses. God will not assign a purpose that you are unable to complete. God assigned your gift before your conception. Our Heavenly Father is extremely knowledgeable of His children. Trust me, we cannot fool him.

He knows when I will procrastinate before it happens. This is when my friends push me. God created my purpose to align with his. That's how dope God is to me.

Secondly, we must know who we are in life. Do you know? If not, dig deep to define your representation. Who we are is connected to our purpose. For instance, I'm a giver. I want people around me to feel good. I want to shower friends and family with encouraging words every time we connect. I always speak life over everyone that is connected to me. I provide words to heal those needing reassurance. I've written many notes, poems, affirmations, and essays filled with beautiful words that would elevate their mood. I want every encounter with family and friends to have a positive meaning.

Thirdly, surround yourself with compatible people. People harmonious in thoughts can compel each other to be the best. You need people who will challenge your process to God's purpose. Everyone has tried to run solo without using God's path. I have tried it. My own process failed every time. I have friends who will remind me, "This is God's purpose for you." It's not about you. Follow directions so God's vision can be fulfilled without interruptions. I need those friends to keep me on my journey. I have days when the spirit of defeat tries it. However, my friends are there to push me further. I appreciate them tremendously. My winning season is destined only by God. This life isn't mine. My life belongs to God.

Fourthly, honor God's journey for you. Don't waste time thinking the process should be perfect. Start and perfect the process as each step is created toward your path to your winning season. Your purpose is your winning season.

Motivation Notes

- 135 -

Isaiah 41:10 "So do not fear, for I am with you; do not be dismayed, for I am your God. I will strengthen you and help you; I will uphold you with my righteous right hand."

Motivation Notes

Isaiah 41:10 "So do not fear, for I am with you; do not be dismayed, for I am your God. I will strengthen you and help you; I will uphold you with my righteous right hand."

Motivation Notes

- 137 -

Isaiah 41:10 "So do not fear, for I am with you; do not be dismayed, for I am your God. I will strengthen you and help you; I will uphold you with my righteous right hand."

CHAPTER 6

Illness

Illness

noun

ill·ness   ˈil-nəs

Synonyms of illness

a: **SICKNESS SENSE 2**

b: an unhealthy condition of body or mind

Life always seems to throw us a curveball when we least expect it. It becomes a double whammy when told our bodies are being attacked by an illness. No one is immune from receiving life-changing news caused by an illness. I have been met with health challenges myself.

Five years ago, I was diagnosed with Type 2 diabetes. I was floored but not surprised because diabetes runs in my family. My maternal grandmother's leg was amputated because of this horrific disease. I did not take my diagnosis seriously until 2022, when my hemoglobin A1C value was 10.4. It was out of control. My doctor sent me a message saying my sugar was too high. I needed stricter diet control. A couple of months later, I was taking Metformin and Ozempic. I would take Metformin daily and give myself Ozempic weekly using a syringe. That was it for me. Now, I needed to use needles to control this disease. I went into overdrive to get in shape. I ate properly and worked out five days a week. I lost twenty-two pounds, which ultimately moved my rating down to pre-diabetes. I was thrilled at my results. This was a game-changer for me. I know my health challenge is minor compared to those who can't change their illness with a simple diet change. I relied on God to keep me obedient. Many prayers and self-reflection allowed me to change my eating habits.

There are millions of people who cannot change their illness with a dietary change. I have friends and family members who battled cancer. Some survived their cancer battles with ease and grace. But I also have friends and family members who died from cancer. Faith must be at the center of our life when faced with a diagnosis that puts an overcast on our life or of the people we love. Matthew 21:22 states, "And Whatever you ask in prayer, you will receive, if you have faith." I have prayed for myself and others to become healthier. It has been a long road to remove diabetes from my body and suppress my appetite for unhealthy foods. Be ready for what you ask God in your prayers. We must pray for relief and healing and be ready to put in the work to defeat any illness that is presented to us.

Prayer for Illness

Heal me, oh Lord, from everything that is afflicting my body. Fill my body with your blessings. Carry away the pain. Move any disease that was attached to my mind or body. Make me whole again. Let me be cleansed with your blood. Repair me, recreate me, and give me strength, for you said, "Ask and it will be given." Father God, I come before you in the need of your blessings.

In Jesus' Name. Amen.

Illness - Check-In

Are you navigating through any health challenges?

If so, create a plan to maintain a positive mindset.

"You can conquer everything that tries to take you down. If only you believe, God will lead you out of the midst of your storm. He will guide you to brighter days. No more pain or sorrow will follow you. Just trust God. He will always cover you. In Jesus' name!"

"Know as you start this journey, God responds to ALL prayers. He's a healer. During these moments, He wraps His arms around us to ensure we are comforted and aware of His presence. I stand with you in prayer and agree no weapon shall form or prosper over you. You are God's child that will tear this disease up. We won't dare say its name, but know your will is already done. Your fight has already been won. We just need to complete the lap to Victory. In Jesus' name. Amen! You got this."

Illness - Check-In

What is holding you back from embracing your new norm?

Describe your journey.

Champion

Who I am today, this person did not exist yesterday. God guided my experiences and destiny as He saw fit. My trials and tribulations were a test of my faith. It was only through my heartache and pain that I became stronger. Now, I can give my testimony. I have not only arrived, thrived, and survived, but I have lived to tell my story as a champion. I have beaten all my contenders. Every enemy that challenged me was beaten by a knockout. God molded me into the champ who stands before you. I'm stronger and wiser because of the many battles I've fought. I thank God for changing me. I thank God for surrounding me with His fortress. I thank God for mending relationships so those can stand with me. You see, I am no longer the person you knew yesterday. Today, I stand here as a champion!

Journey

Your journey was designed just for you. The struggles you've faced only make you stronger. Your undeniable strength defeats all the obstacles that try to distract you. Your phenomenal smile brightens every room when you are dealing with ambiguous situations.

Your voice is a blessing provided by our divine Father. You have power in your tongue. Continue to speak life over yourself. Belt out these self-affirmations daily as this journey continues. When you feel weak, call on our Father to lift you. Trust the process. This will keep you grounded as time goes on. Do not become discouraged, as that is the trick of the enemy.

You will rise and walk through this journey with grace. Time is definitely on your side. Through your journey, know God is on your side. When in doubt, just call on him for guidance. He has ordered your steps for this journey. You can see that all your needs are taken care of without falling. Your journey will inspire those to find their true calling in life.

Embrace this journey set before you. Know that you are living your best life, never skipping a beat. I applaud the strength and grace you've shown. Continue to fight this race, as everyone will continue to support you.

I'm Not Ok

I'm not ok. My thoughts are racing, praying to see another day. My body is under attack. I'm not ok. I feel the pain and numbness coming back. I need to be healed. That's a fact! Time is escaping me. I'm praying the Lord's prayer, "Thy Kingdom Come.." God said to ask for anything and it shall be done. I'm praying for a full recovery. I've been calling on God every day. All I can do is pray, pray, and pray. Help me, Father, I hate taking these pills. I keep telling myself this is God's will. I need His saving grace because I'm not ok. I've cried so many nights. Praying and crying out His name, asking for this illness to leave. My body is tired and completely strained. However, as long there is breath in my body, I will still praise His name. My loyalty to God shall not be in vain. I'm not ok. But my faith in God will forever remain.

Test

Find my tears as each one flows from my eyes to the end of my face. I know this fight will only be won with faith and God's grace. I know this is not my end but the beginning of the life He has prepared for me. This is only a test that will create a template for others to use. I thank God for allowing me to provide these tools. I can't ask for much more. Through all of this, the gift of life is most that I will adore. I'm ready to walk through each door God has opened just for me. This test isn't for the weak. Only the strong shall survive. Walk with me, and you will see.

Illness - Check-In

Are you asking God to heal you?

Write down scriptures that will help you.

____

____

____

____

____

____

____

____

____

Heal Me, Oh Lord

Heal me, Oh Lord. I am lost without you. My mind is imprisoned with stressful thoughts. Give me the strength to push forward. I know you will deliver me. I am depending on my faith to see this through. I've been praying that you will set the disease free. Heal me, oh Lord. My miracle is coming for the world to see. You shall supply my every need. My prayer warriors have all agreed my body will be healed. No more pain shall my body feel. This diagnosis will never hold me back. Heal me, oh Lord. I'm going to be brave because my body will be healed and saved. My mouth will praise your name every day. I feel your blessing coming my way. I'm relying on your grace to fill up my space. Give me peace to sustain my life. You gave your only son for me. He paid the ultimate price. Heal Me, oh Lord.

"Never doubt your journey because this experience will strengthen your connection with God. He will supply all your needs with blessings beyond measure."

Illness Notes

- 150 -

1 Corinthians 6:19-20 "Do you not know that your bodies are temples of the Holy Spirit, who is in you, whom you have received from God? You are not your own; you were bought at a price. Therefore honor God with your bodies."

Illness Notes

1 Corinthians 6:19-20 "Do you not know that your bodies are temples of the Holy Spirit, who is in you, whom you have received from God? You are not your own; you were bought at a price. Therefore honor God with your bodies."

Illness Notes

1 Corinthians 6:19-20 "Do you not know that your bodies are temples of the Holy Spirit, who is in you, whom you have received from God? You are not your own; you were bought at a price. Therefore honor God with your bodies."

CHAPTER 7

Love

love

noun /ləv/

a: to hold dear: CHERISH

b: to feel a lover's passion, devotion, or tenderness for

Love is one of the greatest gifts from God. I experienced the best love by being a mother. There is a magnificent feeling of being a nurturer. My kids taught me that I could provide unconditional love. It has been an amazing journey loving my children. I thank God for trusting me with His special cargo. There can be unconditional love in romantic relationships. Unfortunately, I have never experienced that kind of love in a romantic relationship. Have you been in a romantic relationship that provided unconditional love? If not, be patient; it will happen. However, you must be open to receiving it. Love is the best feeling, especially when it is reciprocated.

When God ordains a love that is destined for two people, anything is possible. It does not matter how the relationship began but how it started with love. God has planned our lives before conception. He knows of all the love and heartbreaks we will experience. It's that special love solely created for His children that will last. I've spent years trying to find that unconditional love only to find emptiness because the love I searched for was not there for me. Ultimately, I figured out that it wasn't love but lust. I've dated guys who checked almost all the boxes, but there was always something missing. Dating has been a gamble for me.

I'm not alone in feeling like dating is like shooting craps. I decided to buckle down to concentrate on myself, finding a closer connection with God. Experiencing true love is all in God's timing. I've patiently waited for the experience of loving unconditionally.

I've heard God's voice several times, warning me to pull back from relationships that were not for me. Did I listen to God's command? Course not. That's why I need to sit still for the unconditional love that was created for me to seek me. Only God can guarantee a mate that will be your partner for life. Genesis 2:18 says, "The LORD God said, "It is not good for the man to be alone. I will make a helper suitable for him."

Prayer for Love

Thank you, Father, for sending unconditional love my way. I'm truly blessed to experience a love created just for me. Your love for me serves as an example. You always love me even when I have failed you. You continue to send blessings that were sketched for me. I'm thankful for my purpose partner. I can combat the wars that rise up against me with my warrior. I know this moment of surrendering to love was orchestrated by you. Father God, thank you for preparing me. Thank you for conditioning my mind, body, and soul for this unconditional love.

In Jesus Name. Amen.

Struggle Love

Who wants to struggle with love? I don't... Love should not be hard. There should be an easy flow between two people. Relationships are both give and take. The problem occurs when there is an imbalance in the work to manage the relationship. That does not mean there should be a 50/50 split. When you do not give love your all, it creates an unstable setting. Two people must love hard and work hard for it. That's the only way to avoid struggling with love.

Dear Heartbreak,

I've been in agony, feeling overwhelmed because someone failed to love me as I desired. You have been in and out of my life for years. When are you leaving? I am counting the days that you will finally exit my life. I've stewed in my hurt for too long. I can never find my way back up. Heartbreak, I never want to see you again. I've been fighting for love for years. Only God and I can count my many tears. I pray that this pain in my heart will end. I'm so confused about love. I don't know where to begin. You've caused me grief. I've cried so many times. Most nights, I could not sleep. I've played this hurt over and over again in my head.

Dear heartbreak, when will you end?

"We are only human. Don't fret about the past. Mistakes will be made until our last breath. Move forward. Understand you are a queen. Don't let this one mishap stop you from opening your heart. Stop stirring in your pain. Your gift was crafted just for you. He is waiting and praying for you at this moment. God will order His steps. He will appear from the shadows to lighten your soul."

"Hurt people tend to hurt others when their pain isn't addressed. If you are hurting, work on yourself before involving people's feelings. Get the help you need to heal your pain."

Are you struggling to let go? When someone shows you who and what they are, believe it. Actions ALWAYS provide the truth about a person's character. Why should you waste time on someone who lacks the ability to love you properly? You were created to be loved unconditionally. Let go of anyone that stains your heart. Focus on loving yourself. Free your mind, heart, and soul from the travesties you experienced in the past. Move forward and onward to letting love swarm its way back into your life. Love is waiting for you. However, to finally have unconditional love, stop tolerating the intolerable!

"Love is like a butterfly; it comes in many shapes and forms. It can be tantalizing, annoying, smothering, and distant. But most times, it's invigorating when the love is returned. Feelings can corrupt one's hope for love, especially when feeling loved is unknown. But trust me, loving and being loved is an exceptional love that will always be known to those who understand it but also welcome the reciprocal part of being loved."

"Heal your broken heart. It was damaged from the start. You walked through life gifting hurt and pain because your life was stained. Take time to heal. Your pain won't stop until there's a mending of your past. Heal your heart, and stop letting the devil pull you apart."

"There's love waiting for you if you just open your heart."

"Stop holding on to people that God blocked for you! Move forward. God has greater replacements."

Love - Check-In

Do you celebrate the power of love? List relationships in your life that represents the power of love. Describe why.

____

____

____

____

____

____

____

____

____

I Am Enough

I am fulfilling someone's dreams by being their wife.

I am not subtle. The mere sight of me is stirring someone's soul.

My beauty is more radiant than he's ever seen.

My scent captures his spirit as I walk by.

I am looking at my perfectly designed body that God created just for his eyes.

He watched me sway from side to side. This walk is only for his sight.

I was created just for one. God has given me treasures only the man destined for me can uncover.

I am enough for the man God has chosen for me.

"Committing to the desires of your heart isn't always smart. Sometimes, you come across someone who will tear it apart. Just know when it's all said and done, it's your mind that will pull the pieces together at once."

Love - Check-In

Do you love yourself? Describe the best version of you.

Gift of Love

Love is a gift that most fail to experience because of their own misunderstanding of "what it is." Finding true love sometimes escapes us due to our "insecurities." Being able to give love sometimes is "intercepted" by our own "self-hate." If we eliminate some of these obstacles, the gift of loving will be given to us. There is a time when you need to understand time waits for no one. Give in, enjoy it, and hold on to loving the perfect partner God has created for you. Lives are forever changed because of the greatest gift. Love...

"If someone cheats on you, don't let your heart stop beating. Breath, smile, and move on to love again."

"Loving again is so real. I finally feel the intimacy that was once misplaced. The pleasure of loving you has filled the empty space. You give me all the joy that I was once denied. Damn, loving you gets better and better with every stride. Loving again makes me high. You, my love, are my ride or die. Keep loving me with every breath. I need this love."

Love Is...

Love is that bright light that shines on you in the morning. The rays from the sun warms your face. There's a glow within that fills every inch of your body. It gives you breath to breathe easy as you lay there gazing into the eyes of the only one you love.

Love is energy that fills your soul with delightful feelings of that chemistry that drives You to soar like an eagle, run through life like a tiger, and fiercely protect your love like a bear. There's no mistake you are full of emotions that have taken over your heart. You have no clue as to why you do things. This is now your new "norm."

Love is smooth when the love of your life caresses your skin. The words that are whispered in your ears melt your soul. It's undeniable you are losing control. This love won't let you wait another second, minute, or hour. This love is so good it's time to devour... I want more of this thing called love.

Love is a fire that eternally burns as you yearn and desire the person who continues to light your passion. They can light your body faster than you can breathe. Every touch and kiss is absorbed. You can't deny this feeling. It's never questioned.

Love is when destined souls understand the blessing of having someone who will stand by your side during the happiest and most difficult times. There's no mistake when God places the perfect person for you in your life. Often, we don't see that love is sometimes hard when the work isn't done. I'm fighting the fight to experience this feeling once again. I'm striving to find what my love is.

"God found two hearts that wanted to love and be loved. Through the years, He shaped and formed your souls to become one. He watched and poured His anointing on you. Time was on your side. He wanted your desires to be met because you have been so faithful."

Releasing You

You were the light to my candle, the star in my sky, the sun that shines its light on me. I felt the love you gave me. It warmed my soul. Somewhere, there was a turn in the atmosphere. You are the darkness in my room. Your light is no longer present. You cut me with your words. Those words transcend everything that is opposite of our love. I've waited for you to emerge from your darkness. I needed you, but you are determined to hurt me. How could you hurt the one you love? I can't continue, so I am releasing you. It hurts me to disconnect, but I have no choice.

I'm clearing my thoughts and soul from you. You gave me no choice. I'm releasing you. You were a waste of my time, energy, and space. You brutally hurt my soul. I don't even want to see your face. Its time. I'm releasing you. I've forgiven you at last. You are my afterthoughts.

The thoughts of our future are in my past. Therefore, I'm releasing you.

Finding Your Worth!

Do you ever question your value? If so, you are not alone. We sometimes doubt our worth in relationships, jobs, or even within ourselves.

Well, the buck stops here. Think about all your pros and delete the cons. I'm sure your pros outweigh the cons. Never second-guess your worthiness.

Years ago, I was locked in a verbally abusive relationship. I dealt with someone who ultimately took my worthiness away with his words. It took a mutual friend to pull me aside to say, "Get yourself together." I didn't care that my weight had ballooned to 184 lbs. My style had lost its luster. I allowed myself to become unrecognizable not only to others but to me.

My confidence was questioned when being compared to other women. You should style your hair like this or try this way to please me. This happened to me in the past. Really? I was baffled because this person was supposed to love me unconditionally. Trust me, there were signs that hit me like lightning in the sky. I went through self-evaluation for years to get the "old Cherice" back. I finally got my groove back. My confidence was back.

I walk into a room and command attention without uttering a word. My aunt always says, "Girl, you are a brick house." I never understood this until I began to appreciate my body. During this time of my self-evaluation, the mirror was my best friend. I would look at my body and smile. I'm not perfect, but I'm perfectly made by God. My 5'6 frame and perfectly sculpted face were created by my Heavenly Father. Why should I continue not to know my worth when God surely did when creating me? I asked myself that all the time.

Listen, keep in mind that you are unique. There is no one like you. We all have our corks, some more than others. Those differences set you apart. Every morning, speak life over yourself. Look in the mirror and recite self-affirmations, meditate, pray, or just sit still and think about all the pros in your life. No one will provide better guidance over your life but you. Whether it's a relationship, job, or yourself that makes you question your worthiness, check yourself right away to avoid a downward spiral. It's hard finding your way back from depths of depression.

Trust me, I know. Life sometimes gives us a box of chocolates, but other times, a bag of rocks. Loving yourself will allow others to see your worth. They won't dare try to question your worthiness if you are armed with self-confidence. My advice is to love yourself tremendously, know your value, and never doubt your worth!

"Finding your light within will help minimize the hurt you feel right now. Remember, man will ALWAYS disappoint us. Only God is perfect! Time and distance will heal your heart. Know that God created you perfectly for this earth. Don't waver from yourself. Keep living in your truth. Don't hide who you are in the future. You are strong, dedicated, hard-working, and phenomenally crafted by God. If your ex can't see your greatness, they ain't the one. It's time out for settling. You are the cream of the crop! You have royalty blood flowing through your veins. God created you in his image."

"God will send someone that will love you just as you are. We fall for people without clearing it with God. Lord knows I'm guilty of it. I promised myself to start clearing my love life with God. I'm so tired of being hurt and being in complicated relationships. I'm asking God to help me define my mate. I've done this by myself for too long. We should never settle for less. I've been through a lot when it comes to relationships. I always choose the wrong person to access my heart. I see red flags, but I continue to proceed. When will I learn? God makes no mistakes. Being in love is a wonderful feeling. Not being loved the same as you love them isn't the greatest feeling. When they can walk away from you, let them walk. Your destiny isn't tied to them."

Finding Love

Finding love was never in my sight. You came to me with all your light. I gathered comfortably in your arms. I feel safe and put together instead of the feeling of being undone. I love you with all my heart. I feel your closeness. Don't ever leave me. I always wanted you from the start. Please continue to give me your space. Damn, I feel so lucky when I see your face. I smile with all my might because you are the one that shines my light.

"Happiness makes life grand!"

Finding Memories

There was a time when we laughed, loved, and cared for each other. Our youth gave our love innocence. We enjoyed walks in the park. It's crazy that every day we were together, we were never apart. It seemed like years, months, days, minutes, and seconds. Our love forever grew. Umph, there were things I never knew. There was this anger in you stirring like a witch's brew. Your words cut me more than a sharp knife. You pour salt on my open wounds, looking at me with hate in your eyes. Damn, what happened? I thought I was your prize. I'm thinking back to the way we were. My thoughts become diluted with the nasty events that continue to occur. My spirit has been battered and bruised. I called on God several times to be removed. I thought this would never end. But God pulled me together. Now I'm able to find memories again.

Storm

When the storm passes by, my world will become dry. I cried so much during the rain as my body felt limp from enduring so much pain. I never thought my eyes would shed a tear. But all the time, my heart dropped whenever you called me "Dear."

Our relationship was more like a storm. It was covered with strong winds and thunderstorms. I loved you more than life. I didn't think twice when you asked me to be your wife. The storm covered our time. I never knew you would cheat and never give our kids a dime. The storm almost swept me away. But God came and saved the day. My storm has ended now. I look back at all your mishaps and say wow. You almost took me out. You yelled, screamed, and shouted horrible things that made me scared.

The devil tried to take my life, but then I heard you call me "Dear." All those horrible names that rolled off your tongue. I remember calling myself dumb. I took your sorry hand in marriage, but I know it's hard to bear me leaving as you thought the end wasn't near. The storm taught me so much. I can overcome anything the devil touches. The storm has passed in my life. No more strife, and, by the way, no more being your wife....

Soul Ties

Undeniably, you are linked to me. Our love is greater than the eye can see. Our hearts, souls, and minds are united as one. No man can put asunder what God has already done. Your lips speak only kinds and sweet words that will forever be engraved in my DNA. God brought us together because that was His final say. I prayed many times for this love to come. We are forever connected molded together as one. Every fiber of our souls is twisted in knots. We are matched eternally. No one can ever fill the other's spot. There's no letting go. We are forever bonded in this life. Our soul ties will never cause us strife. We will forever love, laugh, and pray. Thank God our soul ties are here to stay.

"If you do not know where your relationship stands, pull back. Loving people in an unknown atmosphere will always bring pain. Step back until you know your status in the relationship."

"Who wants an inconsistent partner? Walk away if someone constantly gives you excuses for not spending time with you. Why wait for them to decide that you are the one? Remember, you are the prize for someone who will consistently show up for you. You will never doubt their love. They will always be intentional with loving you."

"Fear of loving comes from fear of loving ourselves. Fear of finding worthiness in people is from fear of finding worthiness within ourselves. Brokenness is from the fear of feeling whole. Put together your life to overcome all your fears. You are the common denominator. Solve your own equation with self-love."

"Love stories first begin and end with loving yourself!"

Love - Check-In

Are you open to finding love and happiness?

Describe your ideal partner.

____

____

____

____

____

____

____

____

____

Baby Glow

You are the light that brightens every room. I remember rubbing my belly anxiously, waiting to meet you soon. I remember hearing your heartbeat while you patiently waited for your grand entrance. I was so excited to hear the sound. I was overcome with joy, feeling your first flutters and kicks. Remembering that day always put a smile on my face. You have a glow given to you by God that only you could show.

God's path for you was constructed before He placed you in my womb. You are designed to be the best. There will be no boulders, mountains, or storms to disrupt your destiny. You were created to be great! Your thoughts are to be focused on ideas that will transform your life. Gifts given by God will be elevated to another level. No woman or man will be able to undo what's been spoken over your life because your destiny will be forever tied to God.

Letter to My Future Husband

I've been waiting all my life to feel the love that is given by you. You know my every move, what I'm going to say, and how I'm going to say it. You and I walk through this journey that turns us into one. I love how you take my hand and whisper promises that are grand into my ear.

The heat of your breath turns me on. My soul is lifted after every word you utter. I've been waiting all my life for this feeling. I long for this kind of love. This here is priceless. I'm reminded of your love whenever I look into your eyes because I get lost. I have a feeling that is so uncontrollable. I love to love you every day. You are my joy. I dreamt about you all my life. I thought about you all the time. I've longed for this day to come because when I saw you, I immediately knew you were the one. I will follow your lead because God has designed you to be my provider, protector, lover, confidant, and best friend. I know this to be true because God gave me these vows before you were revealed to me. God brought us together. No man or woman will ever break this promise before God. I'm ready for God's destination for us. I love you!

Love Notes

- 177 -

1 John 4:18 "There is no fear in love. But perfect love drives out fear because fear has to do with punishment. The one who fears is not made perfect in love."

Love Notes

1 John 4:18 "There is no fear in love. But perfect love drives out fear because fear has to do with punishment. The one who fears is not made perfect in love."

Love Notes

1 John 4:18 "There is no fear in love. But perfect love drives out fear because fear has to do with punishment. The one who fears is not made perfect in love."